The Thinking Tr

Fun-Schooling with

REPTILES & AMPHIBIANS

Science, Research, Writing, Art, Geography & Games

180 HOMESCHOOLING LESSONS & Activities

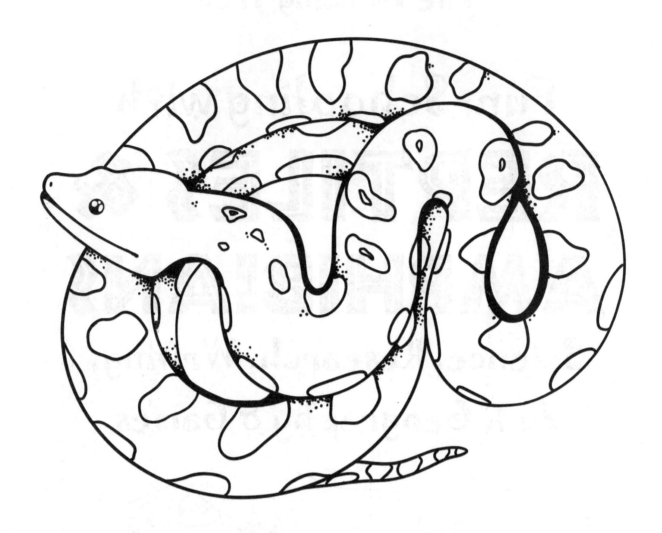

By: Hannah Corey, Abigail Grace Harrison
& Sarah Janisse Brown

We use the Dyslexie Font by Christian Boer

The Thinking Tree Publishing Company, LLC

FUNSCHOOLINGBOOKS.COM

Name:

INSTRUCTIONS

CHOOSE YOUR TOPICS!

What do you want to know about Reptiles & Amphibians?

Draw FIVE things you are curious about:

ACTION STEPS:

1. Go to the library or bookstore.

2. Bring home a stack of at least FIVE interesting books about these topics.

3. Choose some that have diagrams, instructions and illustrations.

SCHOOL SUPPLIES NEEDED:

Pencils, Colored Pencils & Gel Pens.

You will find a Creative Writing Section in the back of this book! Use it anytime!

GO TO THE LIBRARY AND CHOOSE FIVE BOOKS
TO USE AS SCHOOL BOOKS!

1. Write down the titles on each book cover below.

2. Keep your stack of books in a safe place so you can read a few pages from your books daily.

3. Ask your mom or teacher how many pages to do each day in this Journal. Four to Six pages is normal for kids your age. Use one page per day to make this book last one school year!

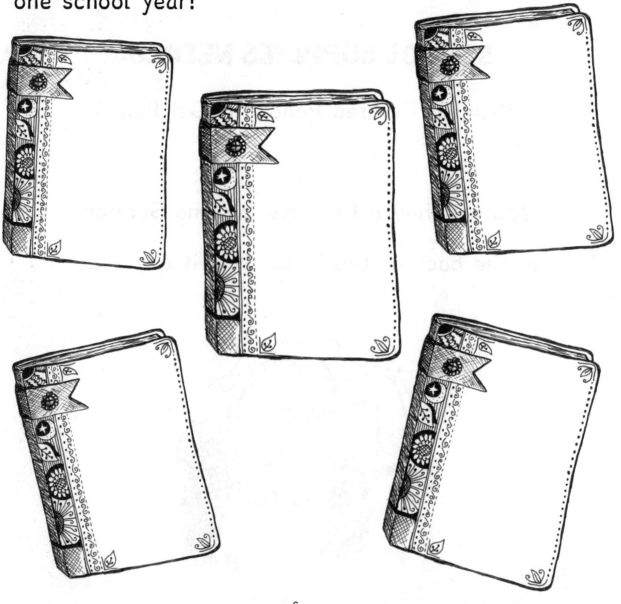

You may choose new books any time.

Flip to the back for more book pages.

Keep all your books in a basket with your pens and pencils.

Have a snack before you start working in this journal.

PICK OUT NEW BOOKS ANYTIME!
DRAW THE COVERS HERE:

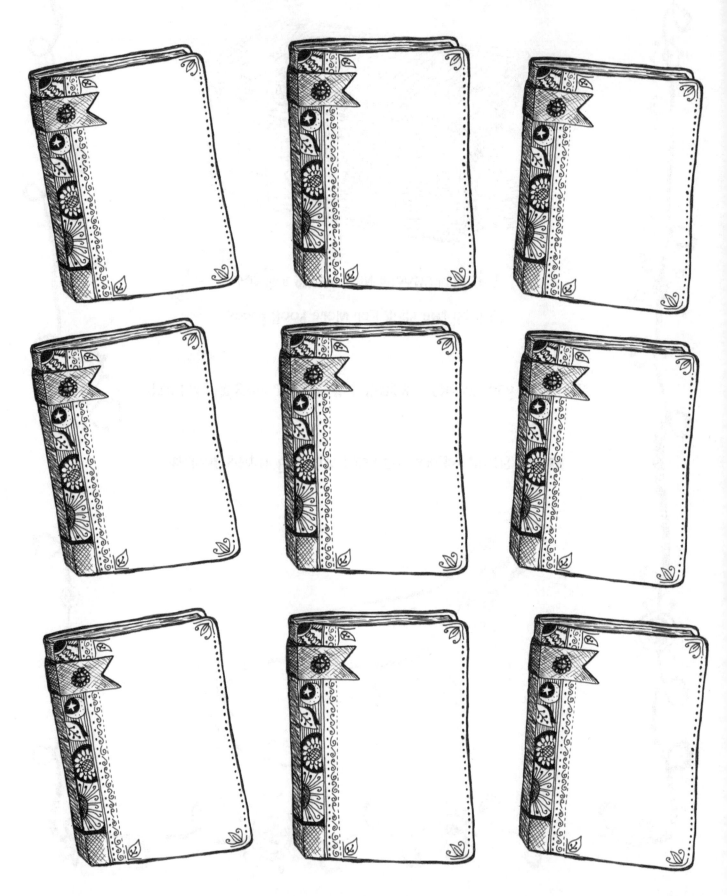

LEARNING TOOLS

My List of Websites & Research Materials:

_____

_____

_____

_____

_____

_____

_____

_____

_____

_____

_____

_____

_____

_____

BABY LOGGERHEAD
SEA TURTLE

DRAW MY HABITAT

RESEARCH!

Look in books, articles or documentaries to learn more about this animal.

HERE ARE THREE FACTS ABOUT THIS ANIMAL:

1. Baby Loggerhead Turtles are called "Hatchlings".

2. Their mom lays the eggs in a hole on the beach. When the babies hatch, they make their way across the sand to the water.

3. When they grow up, they'll weigh up to 350 pounds!

Kingdom	Class	Scientific Name

WHERE IS THIS ANIMAL FROM?

DRAW MY FOOD

DRAW MY ENEMIES

FINISH DRAWING THE PICTURES

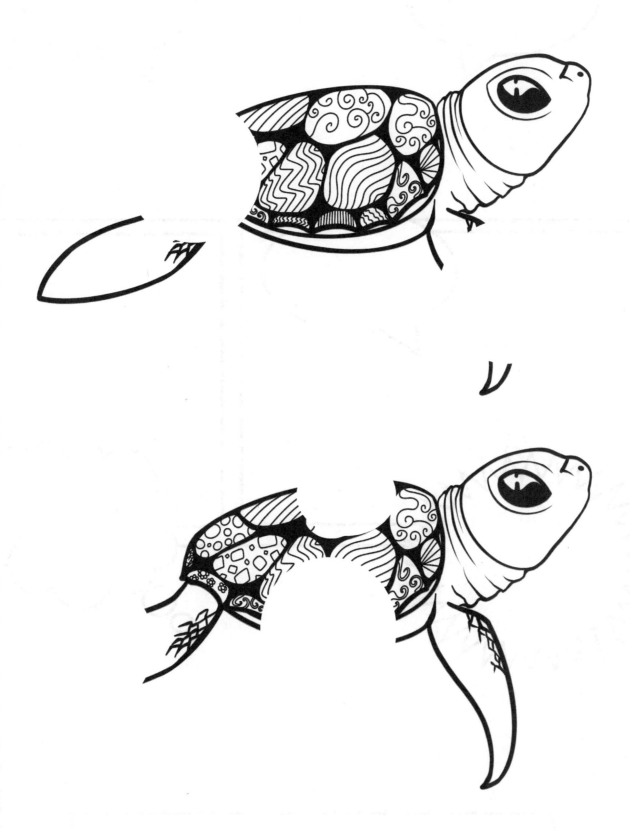

Write a short story about this animal.

_____

_____

_____

_____

_____

_____

_____

_____

_____

_____

RED-EYED TREE FROG

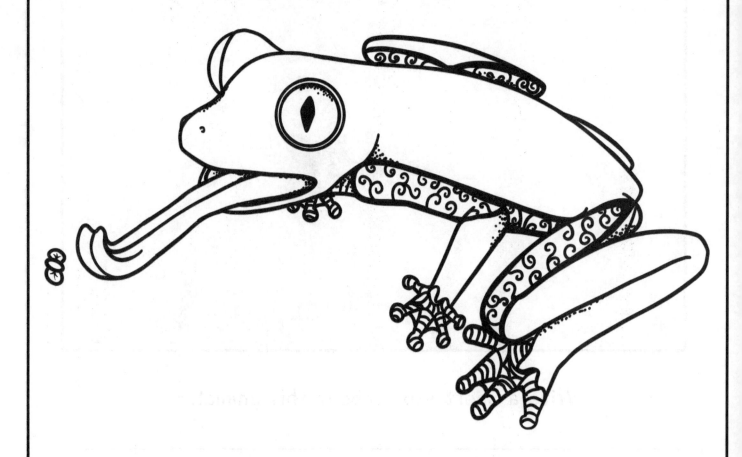

DRAW MY HABITAT

RESEARCH!

Look in books, articles or documentaries
to learn more about this animal.

HERE ARE THREE FACTS ABOUT THIS ANIMAL:

1. They can lay up to **78** eggs at a time!

2. They aren't poisonous.

3. They can be almost **3** inches long.

Kingdom	Class	Scientific Name

DRAW MY HABITAT

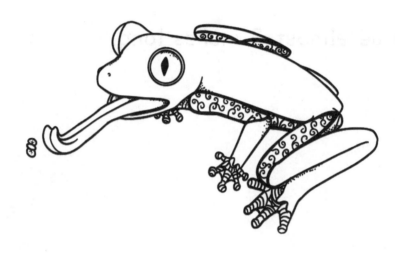

WHERE IS THIS ANIMAL FROM?

DRAW MY FOOD

DRAW MY ENEMIES

CREATE A COMIC STRIP

Write a short story about this animal.

_____

_____

_____

_____

_____

_____

_____

_____

_____

POISONOUS DART FROG

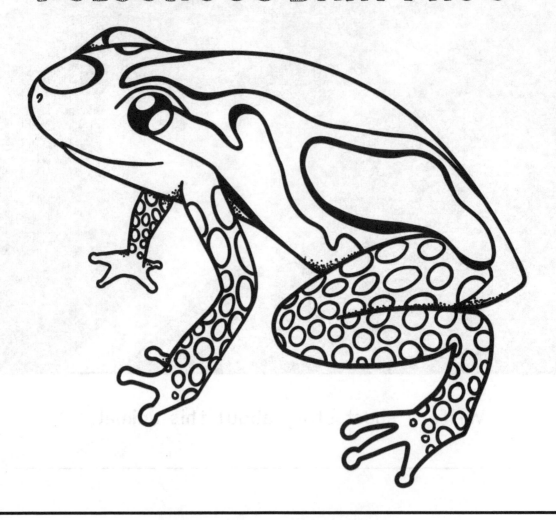

DRAW MY HABITAT

RESEARCH!

Look in books, articles or documentaries to learn more about this animal.

HERE ARE THREE FACTS ABOUT THIS ANIMAL:

1. Poisonous Dart Frogs live until they're **15** years old!

2. The brighter their colors are, the more poisonous they can be!

3. There are more than **170** species of Poisonous Dart Frogs.

Kingdom	Class	Scientific Name

WHERE IS THIS ANIMAL FROM?

DRAW MY FOOD

DRAW MY ENEMIES

CREATE A COMIC STRIP

28

Write a short story about this animal.

_____

_____

_____

_____

_____

_____

_____

_____

GOLDEN TAILED GECKO

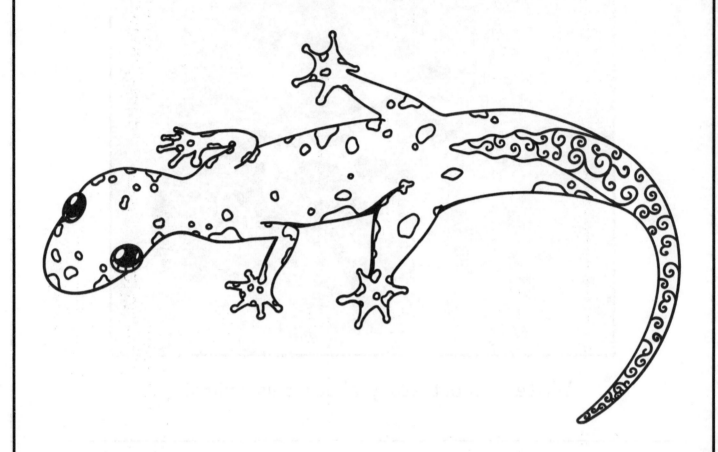

DRAW MY HABITAT

RESEARCH!

Look in books, articles or documentaries to learn more about this animal.

HERE ARE THREE FACTS ABOUT THIS ANIMAL:

1. They are very small, weighing only **0.2** ounces!

2. They have **100%** accurate night vision!

3. They're kind of like a skunk! They have a smelly spray that they use to protect themselves.

Kingdom	Class	Scientific Name

WHERE IS THIS ANIMAL FROM?

DRAW MY FOOD

DRAW MY ENEMIES

CREATE A COMIC STRIP

Write a short story about this animal.

_____

_____

_____

_____

_____

_____

_____

_____

_____

_____

GALAPAGOS TORTOISE

DRAW MY HABITAT

RESEARCH!

Look in books, articles or documentaries
to learn more about this animal.

HERE ARE THREE FACTS ABOUT THIS ANIMAL:

1. They can get up to 6 feet in size and weigh over
570 pounds!

2. They can live more than 100 years!

3. They can go a year without eating or drinking.

Kingdom	Class	Scientific Name

DRAW MY HABITAT

WHERE IS THIS ANIMAL FROM?

DRAW MY FOOD

DRAW MY ENEMIES

CREATE A COMIC STRIP

Write a short story about this animal.

_____

_____

_____

_____

_____

_____

_____

_____

_____

BABY CAIMAN LIZARD

DRAW MY HABITAT

RESEARCH!

Look in books, articles or documentaries to learn more about this animal.

HERE ARE THREE FACTS ABOUT THIS ANIMAL:

1. They can live over **12** years!

2. At 4 feet long, they're considered one of the biggest lizards in the world!

3. Their main predators are crocodiles, snakes and jaguars.

Kingdom	Class	Scientific Name

WHERE IS THIS ANIMAL FROM?

DRAW MY FOOD

DRAW MY ENEMIES

CREATE A COMIC STRIP

Write a short story about this animal.

_____

_____

_____

_____

_____

_____

_____

_____

_____

BABY JAPANESE FIRE-BELLIED NEWT

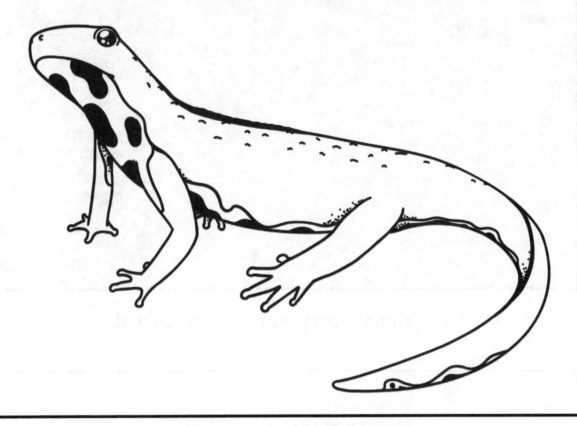

DRAW MY HABITAT

RESEARCH!

Look in books, articles or documentaries to learn more about this animal.

HERE ARE THREE FACTS ABOUT THIS ANIMAL:

1. They have a long tail and fins that make them great swimmers.

2. There are poison glands on either side of their head.

3. They can grow up to **5** inches long.

Kingdom	Class	Scientific Name

WHERE IS THIS ANIMAL FROM?

DRAW MY FOOD	DRAW MY ENEMIES

CREATE A COMIC STRIP

52

Write a short story about this animal.

_____

_____

_____

_____

_____

_____

_____

_____

_____

PANTHER CHAMELEON

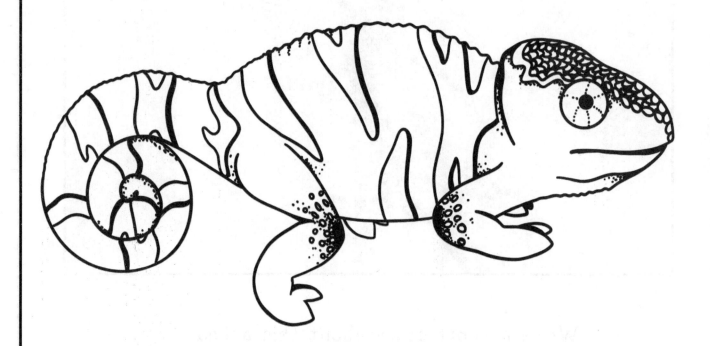

DRAW MY HABITAT

RESEARCH!

Look in books, articles or documentaries
to learn more about this animal.

HERE ARE THREE FACTS ABOUT THIS ANIMAL:

1. They weren't discovered until **1829**!

2. They can change color really fast!

3. Their tongues can move faster than a race car!

Kingdom	Class	Scientific Name

WHERE IS THIS ANIMAL FROM?

DRAW MY FOOD

DRAW MY ENEMIES

CREATE A COMIC STRIP

Write a short story about this animal.

_____

_____

_____

_____

_____

_____

_____

_____

_____

_____

BLUE TAILED SKINK

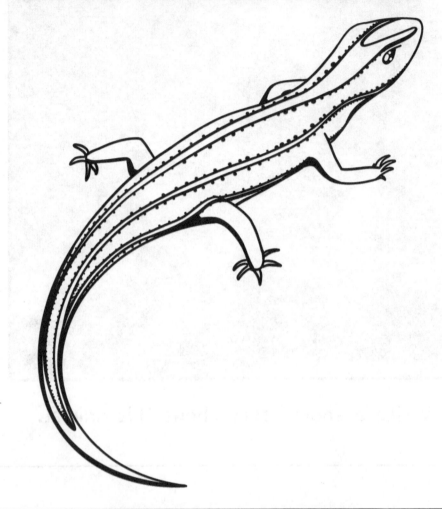

DRAW MY HABITAT

RESEARCH!

Look in books, articles or documentaries
to learn more about this animal.

HERE ARE THREE FACTS ABOUT THIS ANIMAL:

1. Their head is shaped like a snake, and they even have a forked tongue!

2. They lose their stripes when they grow up!

3. They live in the Christmas Islands of Australia!

Kingdom	Class	Scientific Name

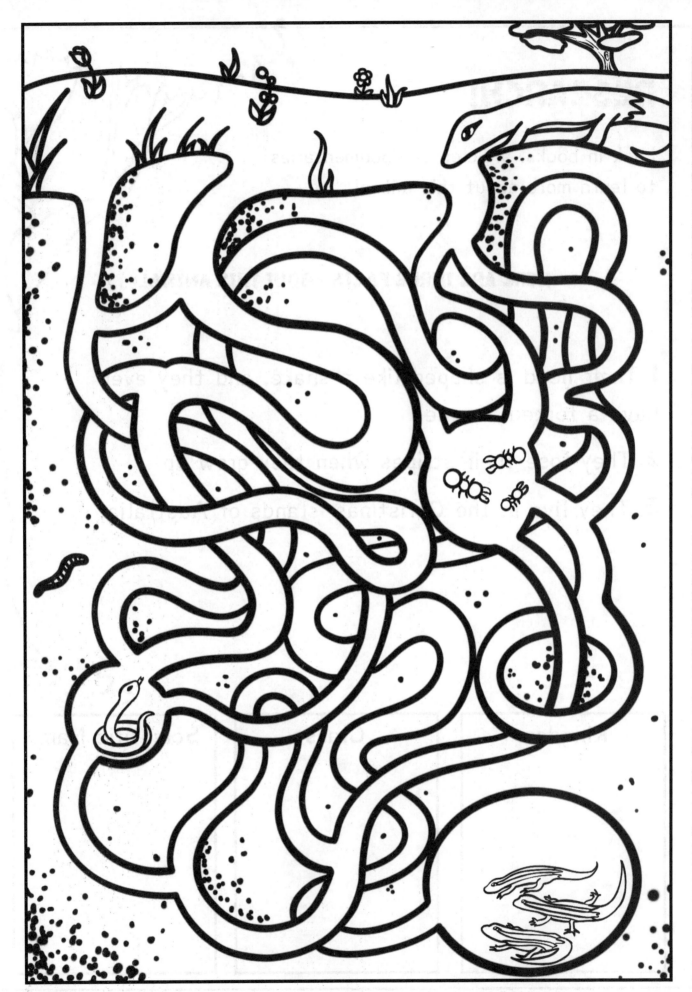

WHERE IS THIS ANIMAL FROM?

DRAW MY FOOD

DRAW MY ENEMIES

CREATE A COMIC STRIP

Write a short story about this animal.

_____

_____

_____

_____

_____

_____

_____

_____

_____

GREEN IGUANA

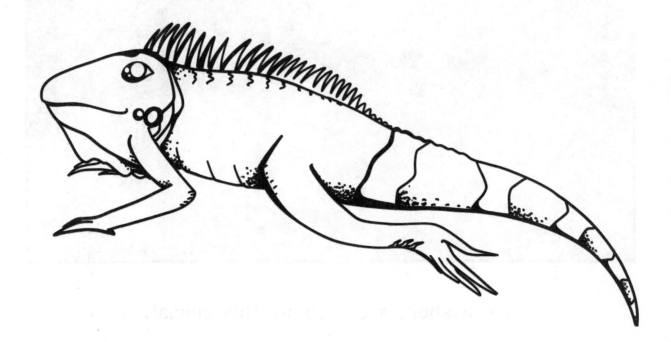

DRAW MY HABITAT

RESEARCH!

Look in books, articles or documentaries to learn more about this animal.

HERE ARE THREE FACTS ABOUT THIS ANIMAL:

1. They can swim really well!

2. Even though they look clumsy, they're actually very fast movers!

3. They stay in the trees and barely ever leave their home.

Kingdom	Class	Scientific Name

WHERE IS THIS ANIMAL FROM?

DRAW MY FOOD

DRAW MY ENEMIES

CREATE A COMIC STRIP

Write a short story about this animal.

_____

_____

_____

_____

_____

_____

_____

_____

_____

KING COBRA

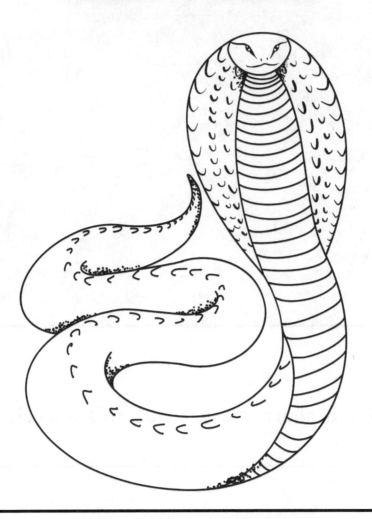

DRAW MY HABITAT

RESEARCH!

Look in books, articles or documentaries to learn more about this animal.

HERE ARE THREE FACTS ABOUT THIS ANIMAL:

1. They are the world's longest venomous snake.

2. They can live until they're **20** years old.

3. Their bites are extremely rare!

Kingdom	Class	Scientific Name

WHERE IS THIS ANIMAL FROM?

DRAW MY FOOD	DRAW MY ENEMIES

CREATE A COMIC STRIP

Write a short story about this animal.

_____

_____

_____

_____

_____

_____

_____

_____

_____

GREEN ANACONDA

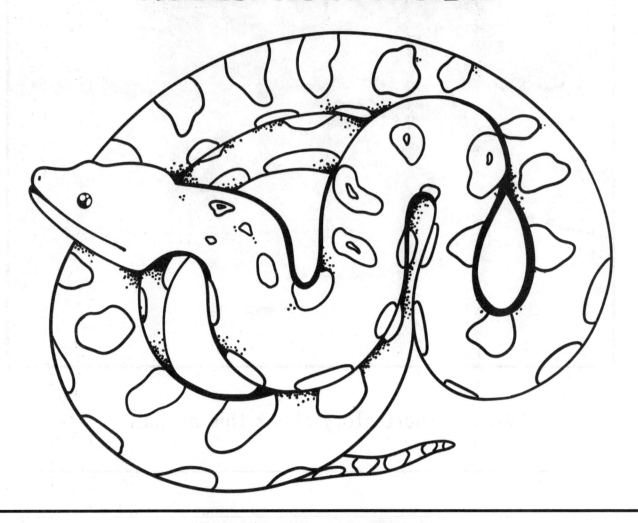

DRAW MY HABITAT

RESEARCH!

Look in books, articles or documentaries to learn more about this animal.

HERE ARE THREE FACTS ABOUT THIS ANIMAL:

1. This is the world's largest snake! It can get up to **40** feet long!

2. Their name "Anaconda" means "Elephant Killer".

3. They are fantastic swimmers!

Kingdom	Class	Scientific Name

WHERE IS THIS ANIMAL FROM?

DRAW MY FOOD	DRAW MY ENEMIES

CREATE A COMIC STRIP

Write a short story about this animal.

_____

_____

_____

_____

_____

_____

_____

_____

ORINOCO CROCODILE

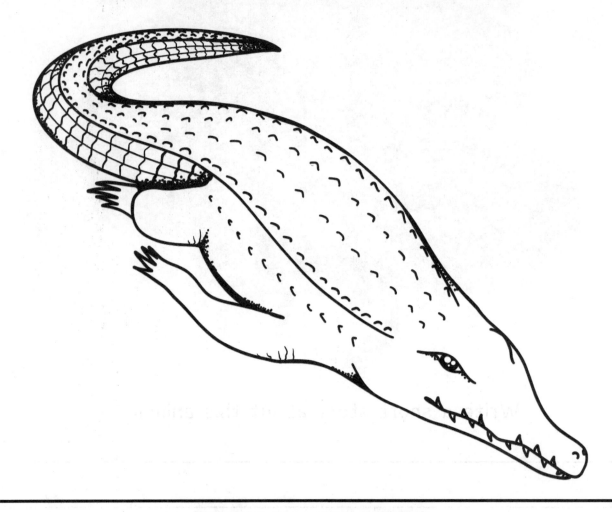

DRAW MY HABITAT

RESEARCH!

Look in books, articles or documentaries
to learn more about this animal.

HERE ARE THREE FACTS ABOUT THIS ANIMAL:

1. They can get to **80** years old!

2. They have webbed feet to help with swimming.

3. They travel in large families of other crocodiles.

Kingdom	Class	Scientific Name

DRAW MY HABITAT

WHERE IS THIS ANIMAL FROM?

DRAW MY FOOD

DRAW MY ENEMIES

CREATE A COMIC STRIP

Write a short story about this animal.

_____

_____

_____

_____

_____

_____

_____

_____

_____

LEATHERBACK SEA TURTLE

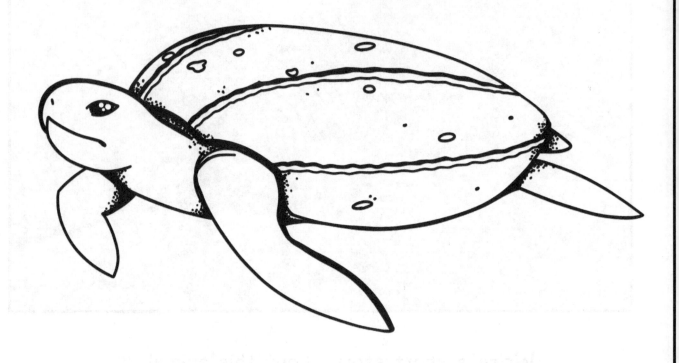

DRAW MY HABITAT

RESEARCH!

Look in books, articles or documentaries
to learn more about this animal.

HERE ARE THREE FACTS ABOUT THIS ANIMAL:

1. They love to eat jellyfish!

2. They grow to weigh more than **11** adult men.

3. They are critically endangered.

Kingdom	Class	Scientific Name

WHERE IS THIS ANIMAL FROM?

DRAW MY FOOD	DRAW MY ENEMIES

CREATE A COMIC STRIP

Write a short story about this animal.

_____

_____

_____

_____

_____

_____

_____

_____

_____

TRUE TOAD

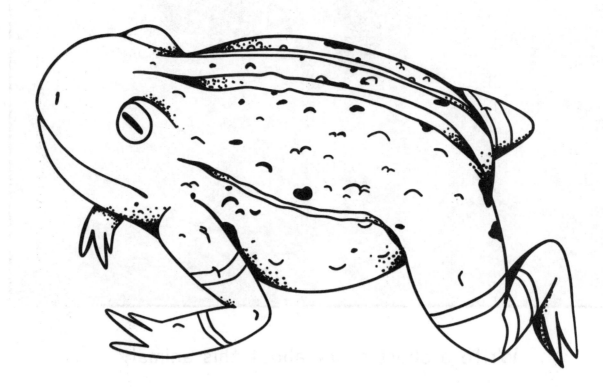

DRAW MY HABITAT

RESEARCH!

Look in books, articles or documentaries
to learn more about this animal.

HERE ARE THREE FACTS ABOUT THIS ANIMAL:

1. They're native to every continent except
Antarctica and Australia!

2. They don't have any teeth.

3. We know of over **6,000** amphibians, and over
4,000 of them are toads and frogs!

Kingdom	Class	Scientific Name

WHERE IS THIS ANIMAL FROM?

DRAW MY FOOD

DRAW MY ENEMIES

CREATE A COMIC STRIP

Write a short story about this animal.

_____

_____

_____

_____

_____

_____

_____

_____

_____

TIGER SALAMANDER

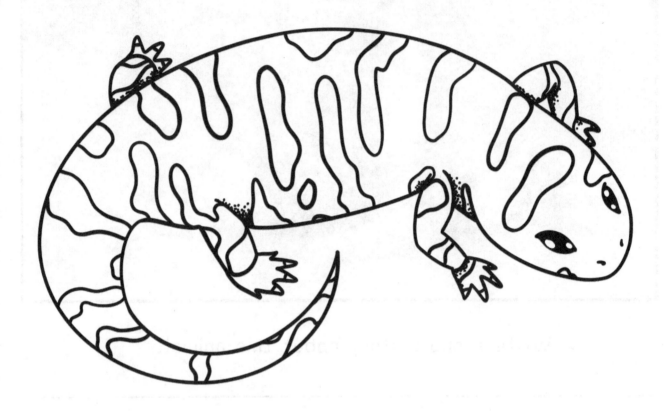

DRAW MY HABITAT

RESEARCH!

Look in books, articles or documentaries to learn more about this animal.

HERE ARE THREE FACTS ABOUT THIS ANIMAL:

1. These salamanders can live **10–16** years!

2. They're otherwise known as a Mole Salamander.

3. They can re-grow any of their limbs!

Kingdom	Class	Scientific Name

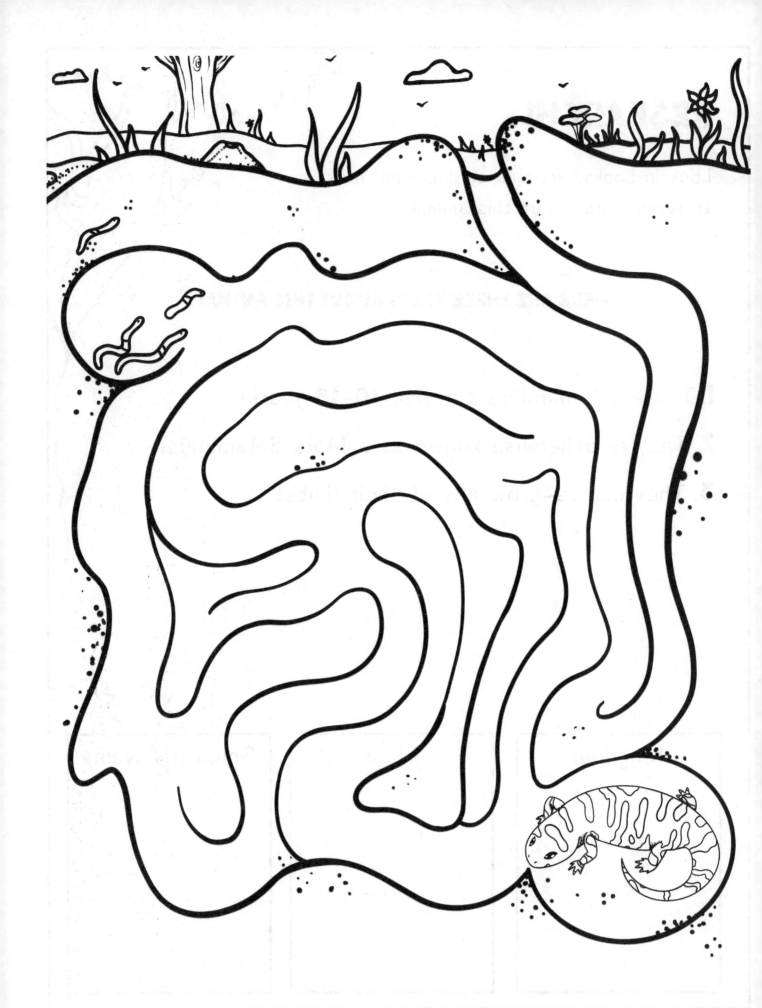

WHERE IS THIS ANIMAL FROM?

DRAW MY FOOD	DRAW MY ENEMIES

CREATE A COMIC STRIP

Write a short story about this animal.

_____

_____

_____

_____

_____

_____

_____

_____

_____

_____

ZIMMERMAN'S POISONOUS DART FROG

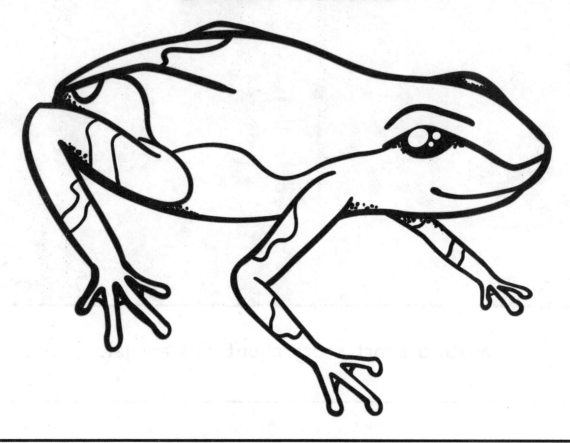

DRAW MY HABITAT

RESEARCH!

Look in books, articles or documentaries to learn more about this animal.

HERE ARE THREE FACTS ABOUT THIS ANIMAL:

1. Their poison is highly toxic!

2. They're otherwise known as the Variable Poison Frog.

3. They can live to be **8-12** years old.

Kingdom	Class	Scientific Name

DRAW MY HABITAT

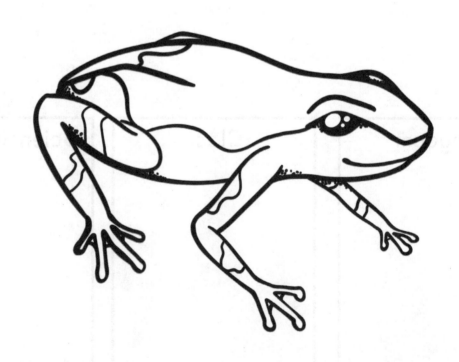

WHERE IS THIS ANIMAL FROM?

DRAW MY FOOD

DRAW MY ENEMIES

CREATE A COMIC STRIP

114

Write a short story about this animal.

_____

_____

_____

_____

_____

_____

_____

_____

_____

CHINESE ALLIGATOR

DRAW MY HABITAT

RESEARCH!

Look in books, articles or documentaries to learn more about this animal.

HERE ARE THREE FACTS ABOUT THIS ANIMAL:

1. They can live to be **50-70** years!

2. They have **17** rows of scales.

3. There are **10,000** Chinese Alligators in captivity, but because of deforestation, there are only **150** left in the wild.

Kingdom	Class	Scientific Name

DRAW MY HABITAT

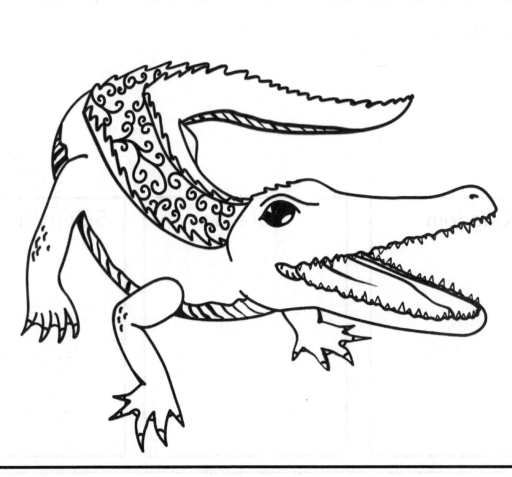

WHERE IS THIS ANIMAL FROM?

DRAW MY FOOD	DRAW MY ENEMIES

CREATE A COMIC STRIP

Write a short story about this animal.

_____

_____

_____

_____

_____

_____

_____

_____

_____

EASTERN BOX TURTLE

DRAW MY HABITAT

RESEARCH!

Look in books, articles or documentaries to learn more about this animal.

HERE ARE THREE FACTS ABOUT THIS ANIMAL:

1. The Eastern Box Turtle is a popular pet!

2. They're about 5-6 inches long.

3. They love to eat berries!

Kingdom	Class	Scientific Name

WHERE IS THIS ANIMAL FROM?

DRAW MY FOOD

DRAW MY ENEMIES

CREATE A COMIC STRIP

Write a short story about this animal.

_____

_____

_____

_____

_____

_____

_____

_____

LEMUR LEAF FROG

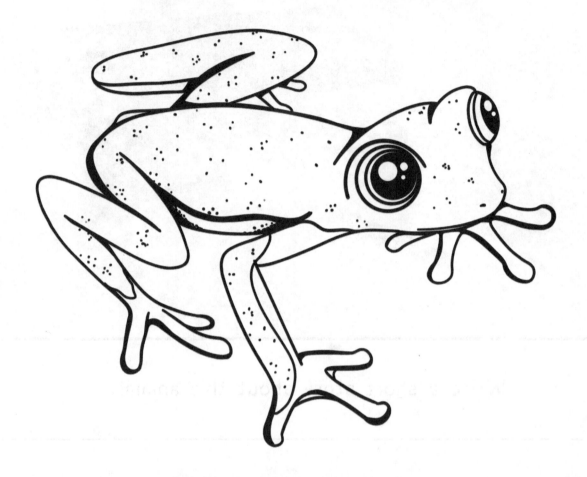

DRAW MY HABITAT

RESEARCH!

Look in books, articles or documentaries
to learn more about this animal.

HERE ARE THREE FACTS ABOUT THIS ANIMAL:

1. They can be found in Costa Rica, Panama, and
Columbia.

2. Male's fight each other for territory!

3. They're endangered because of deforestation.

Kingdom	Class	Scientific Name

WHERE IS THIS ANIMAL FROM?

DRAW MY FOOD

DRAW MY ENEMIES

CREATE A COMIC STRIP

Write a short story about this animal.

_____

_____

_____

_____

_____

_____

_____

_____

_____

SPOTTED TURTLE

DRAW MY HABITAT

RESEARCH!

Look in books, articles or documentaries to learn more about this animal.

HERE ARE THREE FACTS ABOUT THIS ANIMAL:

1. The Spotted Turtle is semi-aquatic.

2. The females have more spots than the males!

3. They will hibernate whenever it gets too cold or too hot!

Kingdom	Class	Scientific Name

WHERE IS THIS ANIMAL FROM?

DRAW MY FOOD

DRAW MY ENEMIES

CREATE A COMIC STRIP

Write a short story about this animal.

_____

_____

_____

_____

_____

_____

_____

_____

_____

CAPE DWARF CHAMELEON

DRAW MY HABITAT

RESEARCH!

Look in books, articles or documentaries
to learn more about this animal.

HERE ARE THREE FACTS ABOUT THIS ANIMAL:

1. When provoked, they inflate themselves and change color so that they look big and scary.

2. They hiss and bite, but they don't have very sharp teeth!

3. Their tongue is twice as long as their body!

Kingdom	Class	Scientific Name

DRAW MY HABITAT

WHERE IS THIS ANIMAL FROM?

DRAW MY FOOD	DRAW MY ENEMIES

CREATE A COMIC STRIP

Write a short story about this animal.

_____

_____

_____

_____

_____

_____

_____

_____

_____

_____

_____

_____

_____

_____

_____

_____

_____

_____

_____

_____

KOMODO DRAGON

DRAW MY HABITAT

RESEARCH!

Look in books, articles or documentaries to learn more about this animal.

HERE ARE THREE FACTS ABOUT THIS ANIMAL:

1. They can run up to **13** mph!

2. When they're scared, they can puke out everything in their stomach so they are lighter and run faster!

3. They can weigh about **154** pounds!

Kingdom	Class	Scientific Name

DRAW MY HABITAT

WHERE IS THIS ANIMAL FROM?

DRAW MY FOOD	DRAW MY ENEMIES

CREATE A COMIC STRIP

Write a short story about this animal.

_____

_____

_____

_____

_____

_____

_____

_____

DRACO VOLANS LIZARD

DRAW MY HABITAT

RESEARCH!

Look in books, articles or documentaries
to learn more about this animal.

HERE ARE THREE FACTS ABOUT THIS ANIMAL:

1. Also known as the Gliding Lizard!

2. People don't mess with this lizard because it
looks poisonous, but it really isn't!

3. They can glide about **26** feet!

Kingdom	Class	Scientific Name

WHERE IS THIS ANIMAL FROM?

DRAW MY FOOD	DRAW MY ENEMIES

CREATE A COMIC STRIP

Write a short story about this animal.

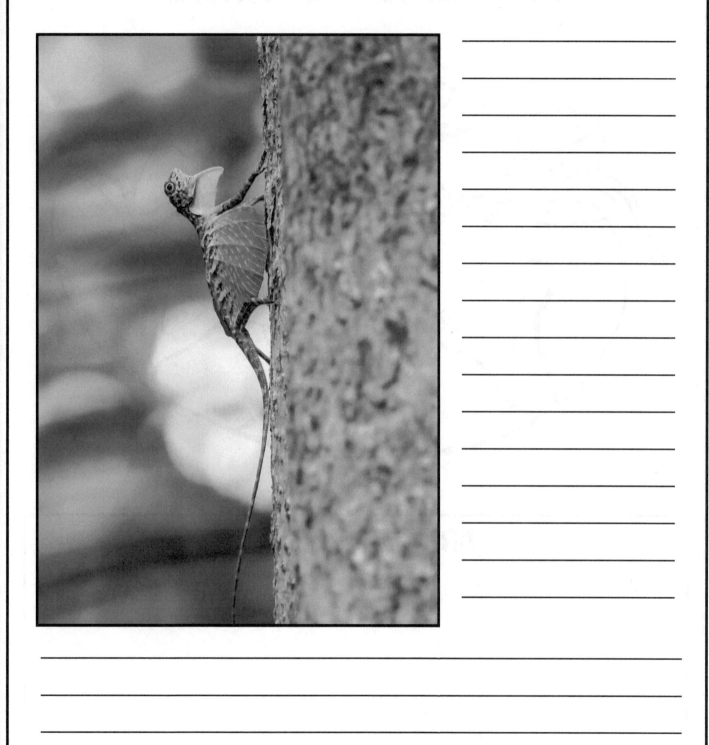

_____

_____

_____

_____

_____

_____

_____

_____

_____

_____

_____

_____

_____

_____

_____

_____

_____

COPPERHEAD SNAKE

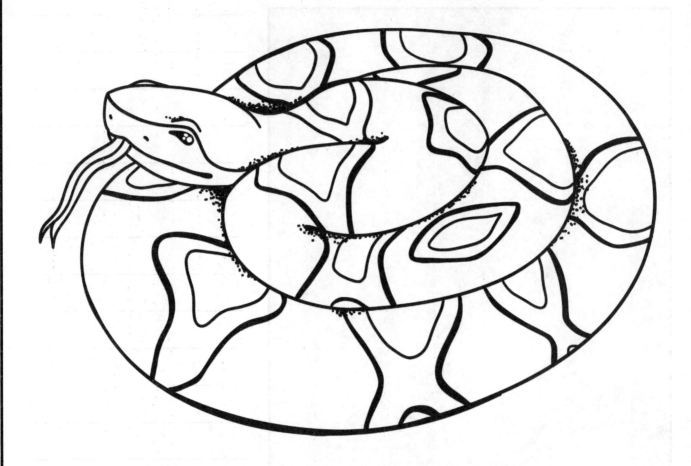

DRAW MY HABITAT

RESEARCH!

Look in books, articles or documentaries to learn more about this animal.

HERE ARE THREE FACTS ABOUT THIS ANIMAL:

1. They're usually **2-3** feet long.

2. They can live for up to **18** years.

3. Young snakes have yellow-green tail tips.

Kingdom	Class	Scientific Name

WHERE IS THIS ANIMAL FROM?

DRAW MY FOOD

DRAW MY ENEMIES

CREATE A COMIC STRIP

Write a short story about this animal.

_____

_____

_____

_____

_____

_____

_____

_____

_____

SCARLET KING SNAKE

DRAW MY HABITAT

RESEARCH!

Look in books, articles or documentaries
to learn more about this animal.

HERE ARE THREE FACTS ABOUT THIS ANIMAL:

1. They can live **10-15** years.

2. They are non-venomous.

3. They eat small mammals, eggs and other

reptiles!

Kingdom	Class	Scientific Name

WHERE IS THIS ANIMAL FROM?

DRAW MY FOOD	DRAW MY ENEMIES

CREATE A COMIC STRIP

Write a short story about this animal.

_____

_____

_____

_____

_____

_____

_____

_____

_____

DESERT IGUANA

DRAW MY HABITAT

RESEARCH!

Look in books, articles or documentaries to learn more about this animal.

HERE ARE THREE FACTS ABOUT THIS ANIMAL:

1. They can withstand extremely high temperatures!

2. They dig burrows, and will sometimes use the burrows of other animals!

3. They don't have predators, but they get run over by cars often!

Kingdom	Class	Scientific Name

WHERE IS THIS ANIMAL FROM?

DRAW MY FOOD	DRAW MY ENEMIES

CREATE A COMIC STRIP

Write a short story about this animal.

_____

_____

_____

_____

_____

_____

_____

_____

_____

DWARF CROCODILE

DRAW MY HABITAT

RESEARCH!

Look in books, articles or documentaries
to learn more about this animal.

HERE ARE THREE FACTS ABOUT THIS ANIMAL:

1. They spend most of their time alone in the water.

2. When in the water, their tails act as a propeller
to help them move.

3. When they're on dry ground they don't just
run— they gallop!

Kingdom	Class	Scientific Name

WHERE IS THIS ANIMAL FROM?

| DRAW MY FOOD | DRAW MY ENEMIES |

Write a short story about this animal.

_____

_____

_____

_____

_____

_____

_____

_____

_____

LEIOLEPIS LIZARD

DRAW MY HABITAT

RESEARCH!

Look in books, articles or documentaries to learn more about this animal.

HERE ARE THREE FACTS ABOUT THIS ANIMAL:

1. They are considered an invasive species in the state of Florida.

2. They make popular pets and can have beautiful patterns!

3. They can be over 7 inches long!

Kingdom	Class	Scientific Name

WHERE IS THIS ANIMAL FROM?

DRAW MY FOOD

DRAW MY ENEMIES

CREATE A COMIC STRIP

Write a short story about this animal.

_____

_____

_____

_____

_____

_____

_____

_____

_____

THE THINKING TREE, LLC
FUNSCHOOLING.COM

Copyright Information

Contact Us:

The Thinking Tree LLC

317.622.8852

Contact@FunSchooling.com

Made in United States
Troutdale, OR
01/05/2025

27645208R10106